Can You Hear Me Now?

Marie Moser

BookLeaf
Publishing

Presentation by *BookLeaf Publishing*

Web: www.bookleafpub.com

E-mail: info@bookleafpub.com

ISBN: 9789357619448

First edition 2023

This is for all my stalwart friends and family who have far more faith in me than I do in myself.

The Place

There is a place I go.
A place no one has ever been or will ever be.
A place I know as well as my own heartbeat but
can never stay.
It is a place of joy, extreme love, dank cold pain,
naked fear and so alone.
My solace is the pain: deserved pain I inflict.
On myself.
On others.
Echoes flash like photographs through my being.
Photographs of laughter,
a forgotten kiss.
Family.
Echoes of a reality that was false.
Only this place remains.
Satisfaction is my comfort.
I Won.
I know not what it may be that is won, but it is
mine.
Every grain of truth is surrounded by an ocean
of lies until it is changed forever.
No one remembers it the same.
Was it the dress she was wearing or the sunny
warmth on my naked back?
And yet I must go.

This is not forever-never has.
Now the cruelty is realized.
All that was sacrificed
so far away, but real.
Never to be accepted,
not even here.
screaming,
WHISPERING
in agony.
It will never change.
Freedom is lost,
forever is lost.
There is only now.
And you have never really known.
And I have never really been.

Love, Strength, Forever

I never dreamed that I would meet
someone as sweet as you.
And now I know forevermore,
there'll be not one, but two.
Two hearts, two souls, two people's love
sharing all we've got.
Knowing that we have a love
that never could be bought.
Two shooting stars colliding
with the force to meld our souls.
And now we've come to realize
that together we are whole.
No more will life be bleak or dark,
as love has lit our hearts.
And now, my Darling, we shall
hold each other and not part.
For we have trudged alone and scared
along the road of strife.
And we will overcome them all
and give each other life.

Story of My Life

Woke up this morning
A fantastic disaster.
Am I wearing pants?

I Will Carry You

When the darkness falls,
and the moon casts its face upon you,
know my security.
When the rain pours down
and the puddles threaten to drown,
know my strength.
When the wind destroys your serenity,
know my peace.
When despair calls on you
and belief is fading fast,
know my hope.
When your heart feels abandoned,
pitched in to the dank and cold,
When you feel there will never be warmth
again...
When you are on the edge
and cannot find your way home;
Hear my voice, hearken my call,
And know my love.

Did The Big Brown Bear
Bring Back Bacon?

Aliens come to my hometown and
Crash the incipient baggage
which was attached by a silky thread of lost life
and bowling.
Feeling low
like a carrot,
Running on to her waiting armies.
Driving galoshes wet,
steering wheel driving.
Drifting along
On a sunset of glorifying gauze,
Reeling the waves,
Cutting the rage,
Raping the whale of translucent realms
and Bearing the Holy Days of
manly gifts.
Running on a wheel of my own understatement.
Feeling like a little girl
and screaming out a
Hosanna to the rest of my tree.
One is one is good is the better
to see my paling sheik and horse of pristine ivory.
See my run.
And fear me alone.

Cheese: More Than Just A Clever Adhesive?

A million words ago, my stamina to fashion compendious phrases, and excogitate long-winded idealistic interpretations was incalculable.

A thousand words ago, my fortitude to contrive concise maxims, and devise obscure lofty analysis was infinite.

A hundred words ago, my strength to create pithy sayings, and think up vague great reasoning was endless.

Today, I had lunch.

Disconnection

You know I love to love you,
My heart is in your hands.
I like to think you love me,
Though I don't know where I stand.
We often flail at shadows
And scream into the dark.
We're searching for a meaning
In every cruel remark.
The silence is what kills us,
Perfecting our last dance.
No one else can spill our blood.
We're flawless at first glance.
We can't get off this ride now,
We're vested in too deep.
I don't care if you bruise me,
Just say you're mine to keep.
I'll subjugate my mourning
With a whimper and a sigh.
You know I love to love you.
Even though you make me cry.

Dinner Time

Heat up that charcoal, get covered in flame.
Being a carnivore is the best game.
Sausages, beef and steak, chicken and pork...
Grill 'em and season and get on my fork!
I'm hungry and grumpy, what shall I do?
I know, I'll start up the old BBQ.
Don't really care if you oink, moo or quack
My sizzle addiction'll make you a snack!

Last Chance

I never thought I'd be the one to leave.
If you had told me, I'd have not believed.
I said I'd be the one who would endure.
But for my empty heart there was no cure.
I'd turned a blinded eye to all your ways.
While tears and bitterness filled all my days.
Forgiveness granted, old ways you'd resume.
Not knowing you were sealing your own doom.
Thought I'd be there by your side forever.
Pat your back and think that you were clever.
You had to know that I was not so blind.
You had to know that someday I would mind.
And now alone I stand and must survive.
And now I know I truly am alive.

The Revelation

I have been here before.
This is not the first time.
I have seen these pictures, read these books.
Why can I not remember?
I recall the chilling howl of the night wind
screaming like a caged animal. And the drip drip
of the faulty pipes.
But this room,
these drab brown walls closing in are different.
I can hear voices like ghosts from the past;
MOCKING ME,
Hurting Me,
killing me.
The threadbare carpet burns my knees as I
descend.
Down
    Down
        Down
The fire is consuming me.
The acrid smoke fills my lungs; the dancing
flames lick at my feet.
I will not be defeated!
Rising, victory in my grasp, I have conquered
the inferno.

The pain is crowded away by the trace of
moisture on my lips.
The heavens are opening.
Refreshing, life giving water falls.
Muddy tracks streak down my arms
as I dance once more.
I have won!
No longer am I in death's bony grasp.
I have been here before.
I see it now,
I know.
No longer will I cower, shying away from life,
weak,
helpless,
huddled lonely in the coldest corner of darkness.
I see hope;
Light
Streaking boldly through my dark solace.
I smell life; spring, wet dog, rubber boots.
This is where I win.
I stand proudly on a mountain of hate
proclaiming Love.
Life.
Happiness.
Death will not win.
I will win.
And until that day I shall cry out: I Am Not
Lost!!!

Midnight Mayhem

Another trip, another night.
Too delirious to be polite.
My advocate will score me peace.
My friends will laugh at my release.
No no, you rest, I'll die alone.
The source of pain remains unknown.
Dangling gaps of light and mystery...
Stop asking for my medical history.
You can't even bother to be my savior,
so I lie here and fuzzily judge your behavior.
John Denver protects his pudding guitar.
My drug addled brain only fear the bizarre.
Even wasted all I feel is the vestige of pain.
Are you kidding me!?!? There goes that damned
duck again!
Stop touching my bed or I'll kick your asses.
Please steal me more morphine next time the
nurse passes.
The swamps of Gargamesh reveal the park
ranger.
BC will deliver me up to a stranger.
Numb going down, numb coming up,
my sweet deliverance will arrive in a cup.
I'd actually be great, except for the beeping...

I'm so glad that none of You have trouble
sleeping!
Daylight will bring me a smallish reprieve,
but I still cannot walk when it's my turn to leave.
Harry the carrot will bid me farewell.
I may still return, it's too early to tell.

The Weight

I am not capable of chewing
a hole deep enough
in my foundation
to establish who I am and who I can be.
The darkness invades and shadows plague.
There is no capacity for the fuzzy
that renders my sharp corners sane.
My friends cannot speak
But they scream in my sordid mind relentlessly.
Sex love pain arousal evidence.
There is no boundary for my insatiable
bone-deep desires.
Lost broken agony - alone always and forever
and always.
Lost chances haunt my wake and
rest is an illusion.
I cannot intrude I cannot include.
I own this.
I will cling to the death while I
steadfastly protect the light and inflation of
More Worthy.
This is not their home. I cannot ask for what
I cannot give.
Just one moment of surrender will impale
their hearts.

A fraud a cheat a liar a shattered soul
Heaping blessings on a tainted trust.
Solace in my vessel of torment.
At least I can protect and not partake.
My shelves will shoulder the weight.
Guilt grief, the pillars bear it all.
This rock will not survive.
This is not a choice but a cessation.

For Rolf

I think I'll fall in love with you,
Even though you aren't real.
As long as I can plug you in,
You always will appeal.
You take me to the brink and back,
It's such a sweet ordeal.
I'm never going to give you up.
I like the way you feel.

Little Buddy

Are you dead or alive?
I never know.
You drift and fade and reappear.
Once melded, our souls and lives and hearts
are now strangers.
Our past is all we share, there can be no future
for us.
Are you dead or alive?
Always in my periphery but not my focus.
I cannot shoulder the weight
Of you.
You carry your own water now, in sickness and
in health.
I will survive the absence but
Not the loss.
Are you dead or alive?
Do I really want to know?
Second hand accounts of pain and fear.
One day the phone will ring and I will hear you,
For now.
I know I failed to keep you safe,
My dear friend, I own that, but
Are you dead or alive?
So tired so old so lost so afraid.
We had plans. We had people.

We had life.
Bikes, school, raspberries, tattoos, a bus.
You are with me always now.
You are safe.
And I may rest.

Open Road

Friedrich, take the wheel.
Ruth will ride shotgun.
State after state, mile after mile,
We escape.
You keep us safe, you deliver us in style.
To our homes away from home.
By the time we reach Chicago dinner is ready.
Indiana serves up love and family and rest.
Recharging for our quest.
Kentucky is frantic and frenetic and frenzied.
But, sweet sweet Tennessee...we've found home.
Tom Sawyer opens his arms. Memphis sirens
beckon.
Barges, Beale, BBQ
Muddy waters welcome. We've built our bridge.
But this world is our opportunity.
New York, your crowded busy loudness
Your lights your heights your angst.
Kansas heat tastes so satisfying.
Maine in rain or shine, our fuzzy friends in the
depths.
Oklahoma routes honour the past and the new.
Embraced by no longer strangers.
Death sites, birth homes, lives led, broken roads
Monuments, favours, tour guides, pizza.

South Carolina pigs, Missouri ducks, Rhode
Island sharks.
Miss Mona takes me to the brink.
I don't need a prescription but I could use some
tequila.
Rest stops, world's largest, oldest, highest...
We'll ride this train car to the heights and
Ape our way through the obstacles.
Vegas birthdays buffet, my Dino serenades.
Friends found and lost, love is a gamble.
Arks, Elvis, tolls, tunnels, dinosaurs,
Heights, depths, caves, presidents, a lighthouse.
Power and freedom and disbelief.
You carry our baggage. You make this a reality.
Friedrich take the wheel.

Absence

Sometimes I wish that I had not been born.
Then I would not be sitting here forlorn.
Regretting all the things I've done and said.
Your life would mean much more if I were dead.
I'd appreciate things I never had,
With no emotions here to make me sad.
I'd look at places that I've never seen,
And go to places that I've never been.
Reflective eyes would see all I have known,
And speculate on ways I could have grown.
The people that I love would be no more.
I'd silently but firmly close the door.
The pain, the hurt, the truth would go away.
And from my chosen path I would not stray.
Emotions have no place here in the dark.
I know I never really made a mark.
Unfailingly, I guess I'd been a fool.
Unknowingly, they all had been so cruel.
Unfettered eyes can truly see the light,
For all along I'd know that they'd been right.
Delusions, dreams and hopes can cause one pain.
I know I'll never know the truth again.
And yet I live, my heart is tired and worn.
Sometimes I wish that I had not been born.

I Wish I Knew How

Shall I fear the hate or hate the fear?
Years, Months, Weeks, Days, Hours sacrificed
for the blood lust permeating our survival.
There can be no trust.
There must be no surrender.
This battle will empty our coffers; dry, brittle,
shattered.
Unexpected love, unacceptable control .
Round up, cover up, clean up, close up.
This betrayal changes the dynamic - we cannot
afford to lose.
We have already won.
Solidarity, fortitude, there's freedom in this
prison cell.
No silence, no threats, no malice can drown out
the inexorable demand
for Humanity
Mile after mile.
This unstoppable deafening uproar cannot
Will Not
be subdued or diminished by Inconsequential
depraved instruments.
Their shadows will never lessen our
illumination.
Absolute carnage will be upstaged by

Our Voices.
By our unswerving resolve.
No compromise, no surrender, no victory too
small.
Our tribe is life.
United.
This trial, this false portrayal of a savior,
This loathing of our existence will be
Defeated.
We shall carry the day.
We shall lead the way.
Follow if you dare.

Sorry For Your Trouble

Prowling the edges of life after hours,
Cowering in the corner silent gives me more
power.
Out of body, out of time, out of life, out of
chances;
Peeling me up off the floor with your dances.
Trying desperately to release you of the burden
of me,
But you refuse my attempts to set you all free.
I've got it together, so don't be concerned.
Each text, drink or loss is a lesson learned.
Your lack of trust breaks my fucking heart,
But I know that my life is falling apart.
Waiting for the sunlight of my morning
connection,
Manic panic, my life needs correction.
The sweet, the bitter, small, large, warm and
cold.
I feel naked, open, vulnerable and old.
Blinded by fear but I still clearly see.
You sweet mother fuckers just won't let me be.
Just let me escape and you will be released.
I'm willing to fade away to give you some peace.
I apologize now for taking up space.
I know I do not belong here in this place.

The Hot Dog Song

Hot dogs are so yummy
I roast 'em on the fire.
If you say I don't like 'em
You know you are a liar.

I smother them in ketchup.
They're a delicious treat.
I eat 'em when I'm craving
High caloric meat.

'Cause they're hot dogs,
Yummy hot dogs.
If you've never tried 'em,
Just give them a whirl.

They're tasty, hot and juicy,
Best food in the whole world.
So when you're looking at me,
You're looking at a hot dog girl!

A Mind of Its Own

Turn Here!
Don't eat my jello
Leaf rustlers
Fanny
Pack
Incision Allen gives birth to a
Ghostly Unicorn
Snaps at the Bob Dylan beatnik night
The possum speaks truth
To the rabbit
Open hands open purse open wainscotting open
eavestrough
There goes the oldest Toyota I've ever seen!
You must help
                make
                    hammocks
Annihilate the cannonballs and chocolate
Bunnies
If you want more power, bite a
Frenchman...they're like cinnamon.
They gave us nothing to do
but silence.

You Took Me By Surprise

Romance
Sexy, smooth
Kiss, dance, drive
So girly when wooing
Love

www.ingramcontent.com/pod-product-compliance
Lightning Source LLC
LaVergne TN
LVHW021339200726
843509LV00014B/2588